Pigs

James Maclaine

Illustrated by Jeremy Norton

Additional illustrations by Roger Simó
Designed by Sam Whibley and Amy Manning

Pig consultant: Professor David Macdonald CBE,
Wildlife Conservation Research Unit, Zoology Department, University of Oxford
Reading consultant: Alison Kelly

Contents

World of pigs

There are over 20 different types of pigs.

All pigs have round bodies and large heads.
They have long noses called snouts.

The pigs in this group are wild boars.

On the farm

Lots of pigs live on farms. Farmers keep them for their meat.

Pigs live indoors on most farms. They are kept inside big sheds.

They eat pellets of food from containers called feeders.

They push pipes with their noses and drink water that comes out.

These young pigs live on a small farm.
They spend lots of time outside.

Pigs kept on farms often
have curly tails. Wild pigs'
tails are straight.

5

Wild pigs

There are lots of different wild pigs around the world. They live on grasslands and in forests, deserts and swamps.

This is a warthog. It's a type of wild pig that lives in Africa.

It has four bumps on its face. Long teeth called tusks stick out of its mouth.

A warthog's neck and back can be very hairy.

Warthogs and other wild pigs live where they can find enough food and water.

They need plenty of plants for shelter so they can hide from dangerous animals.

Pig families

In the wild, most female pigs and their young live together in groups.

Up to 20 female and baby wild boars live in a group. They eat, sleep and play together.

Male wild boars live alone. They try to stay away from each other.

Once a year, males visit different groups, so they can meet female wild boars.

Male wild boars sometimes fight over the females.

These males are hitting each other with their heads.

The winner stays with the females for a while.
He will be the father of their babies.

Baby pigs

Mother pigs are called sows and their babies are piglets.

A red river hog sow leaves her group to find somewhere safe and quiet.

Then she makes a nest. She digs a shallow pit and lines it with grass.

The sow lies down in her nest. Soon four to six piglets are born.

These red river hog piglets are just a few days old.

The stripes on their bodies will fade as they grow up.

Warthog babies are born in a burrow under the ground.

Growing up

A mother pig takes care of her piglets.
They spend lots of time drinking her milk.

These piglets live on a farm.
They're sucking milk from their
mother's teats.

Wild piglets stay close to their nest when they're very young.

When they're two weeks old, they start to search for insects and plants to eat.

Piglets keep drinking their mother's milk for three or four months. They drink while she is lying down or standing up.

A mother pig makes grunting sounds, so her piglets know when they can drink.

grunt
grunt

Strong snouts

Pigs use their snouts to smell and search for food.

This wild boar is sniffing the air. All pigs can sense smells up to 2,000 times better than you can.

A warthog digs up plants with its snout so it can eat their roots.

In winter, wild boars can sniff out food even when it's buried under snow.

Some people train pigs to sniff for truffles. Truffles are similar to mushrooms and grow in the ground. They are good to eat.

Pigs eat fruits, seeds, plants, insects and even small animals.

Hairy pigs

Most pigs have stiff hairs over their bodies. Some pigs have more hair than others.

Tiny insects live in pigs' hair. Birds like to eat them.

This bird is hunting for insects on a warthog.

Sometimes pigs show how they feel with their hair.

When a bushpig is scared, the hairs on its head and neck stand on end.

Red river hogs twitch tufts of hair on their ears to show how they feel.

Male warty pigs grow long, spiky hair on their heads to attract females.

Mangalitza pigs have lots of thick, curly hair.

Diving in

Pigs spend lots of time in water whenever they can. All pigs can swim.

Pigs sometimes search in shallow water for plants and animals to eat.

Bearded pigs swim across rivers to reach new places where they can find food.

On some farms, pigs lie in baths of water to keep themselves cool.

These pigs live on a tropical island.
They are swimming in the sea.

Red river hogs swim underwater
to escape from dangerous animals.

Teeth and tusks

All pigs have strong, flat teeth that are good for chewing tough food. Some pigs also have four long teeth called tusks.

Male wild boars mark trees with their tusks to show where they live.

This is a male babirusa pig.

Male babirusa pigs have very curly tusks, but females have none.

Warthogs use their sharp tusks when they fight each other.

These young males are fighting to find out who is strongest.

Most types of pigs have 44 teeth each. People have up to 32.

Muddy pigs

Pigs need mud to keep their skin healthy and their bodies cool.

Pigs often roll in a wet, muddy place known as a wallow.

Then they stretch out to let the mud dry.

The layer of dried mud protects their skin from biting insects and the sun.

These red river hogs are eating mud because it contains salt. Pigs need to eat some salt to stay healthy.

If pigs get mud up their noses, they blow them clean.

Staying safe

Wolves, snakes, bears and big cats hunt pigs to eat. Pigs try to keep themselves safe from these animals in different ways.

These bearded pigs are looking for food when it's dark so other animals cannot spot them.

Adult pigs stand around young pigs in their group to protect them.

The stripes on some piglets' bodies help them to hide in grasses and leaves.

Warthogs try to scare attackers by running at them very fast.

When a pig is scared, it warns other pigs of danger by making smelly pee.

Fast asleep

Pigs sleep during the day and at night. They keep the places where they sleep clean.

These wild boar piglets are sleeping in their nest. They lie next to each other, to stay warm.

Pigs that live on farms sometimes sleep in huts called arks.

Farmers put up hot lamps to keep piglets warm while they sleep.

Some wild pigs sleep in holes in the ground. Others sleep in nests.

Pigs often snore when they're sleeping.

zzzzzz

Noisy pigs

Pigs make lots of different sounds.

Pigs grunt again and again while they're searching for things to eat.

Piglets squeal when they're left alone, so their mother will come to find them.

If a pig spots something dangerous, it barks. This tells the other pigs in its group to run away.

Pigs grunt loudly and rub their snouts together when they meet.

These young pigs are greeting each other.

Glossary

Here are some of the words in this book you might not know. This page tells you what they mean.

 snout - the long nose and mouth parts of a pig's head.

 feeder - a container for food. Pigs on farms often eat from feeders.

 tusk - a long, curved tooth. Only some pigs have tusks.

 sow - a mother pig. Sows live in groups with their young.

 teat - part of a mother pig's body where milk comes out.

 wallow - a wet, muddy place where pigs roll around.

 ark - a low hut on a farm where pigs rest or sleep.

Websites to visit

You can visit exciting websites to find out more about pigs. For links to sites with video clips and activities, go to the Usborne Quicklinks website at **www.usborne.com/quicklinks** and type in the keywords "**beginners pigs**".

Always ask an adult before using the internet and make sure you follow these basic rules:
1. Never give out personal information, such as your name, address, school or telephone number.
2. If a website asks you to type in your name or email address, check with an adult first.

The websites are regularly reviewed and the links at Usborne Quicklinks are updated. However, Usborne Publishing is not responsible and does not accept liability for the content or availability of any website other than its own. We recommend that children are supervised while on the internet.

Piglets spend lots of time playing together.

Index

Acknowledgements

Photographic manipulation by John Russell
Additional designs by Catherine MacKinnon

Photo credits

The publishers are grateful to the following for permission to reproduce material:
Cover © E.A. Janes/age fotostock/SuperStock; **p1** © Santiaga/Thinkstock; **p2-3**
© Bridyak/Thinkstock; **p5** © age fotostock/age fotostock/SuperStock; **p6-7** © Roland Seitre/naturepl.com;
p9 © blickwinkel/Alamy; **p11** © ZSSD/Minden Pictures/Corbis; **p12** © Frank May/dpa/Corbis; **p14** ©
Andy Rouse/2020VISION/Nature Picture Library/Corbis; **p16** © Gallo Images/Gallo Images/SuperStock;
p19 © Tony Pullar/Alamy; **p20** © Minden Pictures/Minden Pictures/SuperStock; **p21** © Philip Perry/FLPA;
p23 © Nature PL/Nature PL/SuperStock; **p24** © Nick Garbutt/naturepl.com; **p26** © blickwinkel/Alamy;
p29 © J.-L. Klein and M.-L. Hubert/FLPA; **p31** © Little Blue Wolf Productions/Corbis

Every effort has been made to trace and acknowledge ownership of copyright. If any rights have
been omitted, the publishers offer to rectify this in any subsequent editions following notification.

Sun, moon and stars

Farm animals

Elizabeth I

Rubbish & Recycling

Dogs

Horses and ponies

Spiders

Planes

Cats

Ancient Greeks

VOLCANOES

DINOSAURS

Your Body

Armour

Sharks

Celts

VIKINGS

Castles

How flowers grow

Digging up the past

Living in space

Caterpillars and Butterflies

Ballet

Pirates

EGYPTIANS

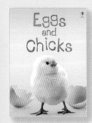
Eggs and Chicks

ROMANS

Weather

Tadpoles and frogs

Why do we eat?

Under the sea

Bears

AZTECS

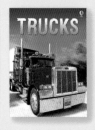
TRUCKS

Night Animals

Firefighters

Antarctica

Bugs

COWBOYS

Planet Earth

London

Seashore

China

Dangerous Animals

Rainforests

Trees

Reptiles

Ships

Bats

Penguins